AF249163

GOING OUT

Written and illustrated by
Lesley Anne Ivory

Burke Books **LONDON & TORONTO**

ISBN 0 222 99316 2 Hardbound
ISBN 0 222 66897 0 Limp
ISBN 0 222 99281 6 Library

Burke Publishing Company Limited,
14 John Street, London WC1N 2EJ.
Burke Publishing (Canada) Limited,
P.O. Box 48, Toronto-Dominion Centre,
Toronto 111, Ontario.
Printed in Great Britain by
T. & A. Constable Ltd., Edinburgh.

Mummy, Pat and Anne
sometimes go to the post box.

Going to the zoo is a treat.

Going shopping is fun too.

When Tim had a cold
he went to see the doctor.

Elizabeth is five today.

The children have come to her party.

Sometimes we go for walks
in the country.

We are in the train.
Guess where we are going!

At the seaside
we play in the water . . .

. . . and on the sand.

"Let's go by bus," says Mummy.

Mummy, Sara and Joan
have a picnic in the woods.

Daddy is taking us to the circus.

We love to watch the clever seals.